Landscaping Lies
On School Drive

AMANDA PERRY

Published by Franklin Publishers

Printed in the United States of America

For permissions, inquiries, or additional copies, contact:

Franklin Publishers

www.franklinpublishers.com

ACKNOWLEDGEMENTS

There are so many people I owe my life to,

Police officers get a bad rap—and some of them lived up to that.

But there were a few.

You know who you were.

You were there for me.

You're still there.

You told me you'd see this through, you'd stand by my side

And ensure the safety of both my self and my children.

Please know how much I value you.

DEDICATIONS

To the Aggressively Fierce Women Who have supported me,

Day in and Day out through all of this

from Emily, Kate, Tanya, Jessica, Amanda, Karen, Sheri, there are so many of you these are just a few of you :

Tanya,

I can't put into words the gratitude I have for you.

You very easily could have chosen to hate me.

Instead, You've held my hand.

In the emergency room, at the police station, in a court room.

You've heard me cry, scream, doubt myself, vent frustration and have seen me at my worst.

You've reminded me of the strength I have.

That together we can fight this, and we WILL protect our children.

You motivated me to put all of this onto paper,

And to no longer live in silence.

I've been quiet for too long.

Thank You,

For simply being you.

Jessica,

You came, the day I called.

I blew off your wedding but you were here for me when I needed you.

So many years you lived down the street but had no idea, the life I was living.

You showed up and helped me pack my kid's bedroom. Listened to everything.

We did jello shots as we celebrated the little wins. Chugged Tito's when we needed it.

Then you stood by my side as I sang my heart out to Kelsea Ballerini on a Saturday night as I healed.

Bubs, Hope, Faith, Grace and Arrow.

You kids.

You do it.

You save me.

Everyday.

-you also drive me absolutely insane and I wouldn't have it any other way

TABLE OF CONTENTS

FOREWORD

Healing, in general, can be tragic or beautiful. You hold the pen and get to dictate just how that process goes.

For years, women have experienced things that are unspeakable and made to feel that somehow it makes us less. That these horrible things that have happened to us are us.

They aren't.

No, Darling, you are you.

You are more than the hideous things you have overcome and you have made it through.

By putting words to the unspeakable things,

I aim to take away the power he holds over you, over me. No longer will you live in shame, no, now you will own the pride and the autonomy over yourself.

They say it takes a Woman, on average, 7 times before she makes it out.

1. In a desperate cry for help, the officer said, "I want what's best for your family, arresting him, isn't it. Go to therapy, man."

2. I called my dad on Mother's Day. He came and took us all from the house. This lasted maybe 2 days?

3. Snuck out of the house with my mother, and went to the court, tried to get emergency custody of the kids. Failed.

4. You were arrested; 2 weeks of jail and a rehabilitation program weren't enough.

5. Arrested again, I moved back to my parents. Filed for divorce and custody. Surprise, I'm back again in 2 days.

6. Back in Jail, another 2 weeks. You're not coming home to me.

7. ....Not happening

And if you're a dude,

DO YOU!

More power to you. I'm so sorry for anything you've been through, too.

This isn't to gender exclude.

So now I invite you,

 join me on my,

first person recount

of the trauma's

I've inhaled.

the worst of the worst

the nights I thought I'd never survive,

 the mornings I didn't want to wake up.

It was through these Landscaping Lies

that I lived

and gained some of the greatest beauties of my life

right on that cursed School Drive.

Preludes & Planting Seeds

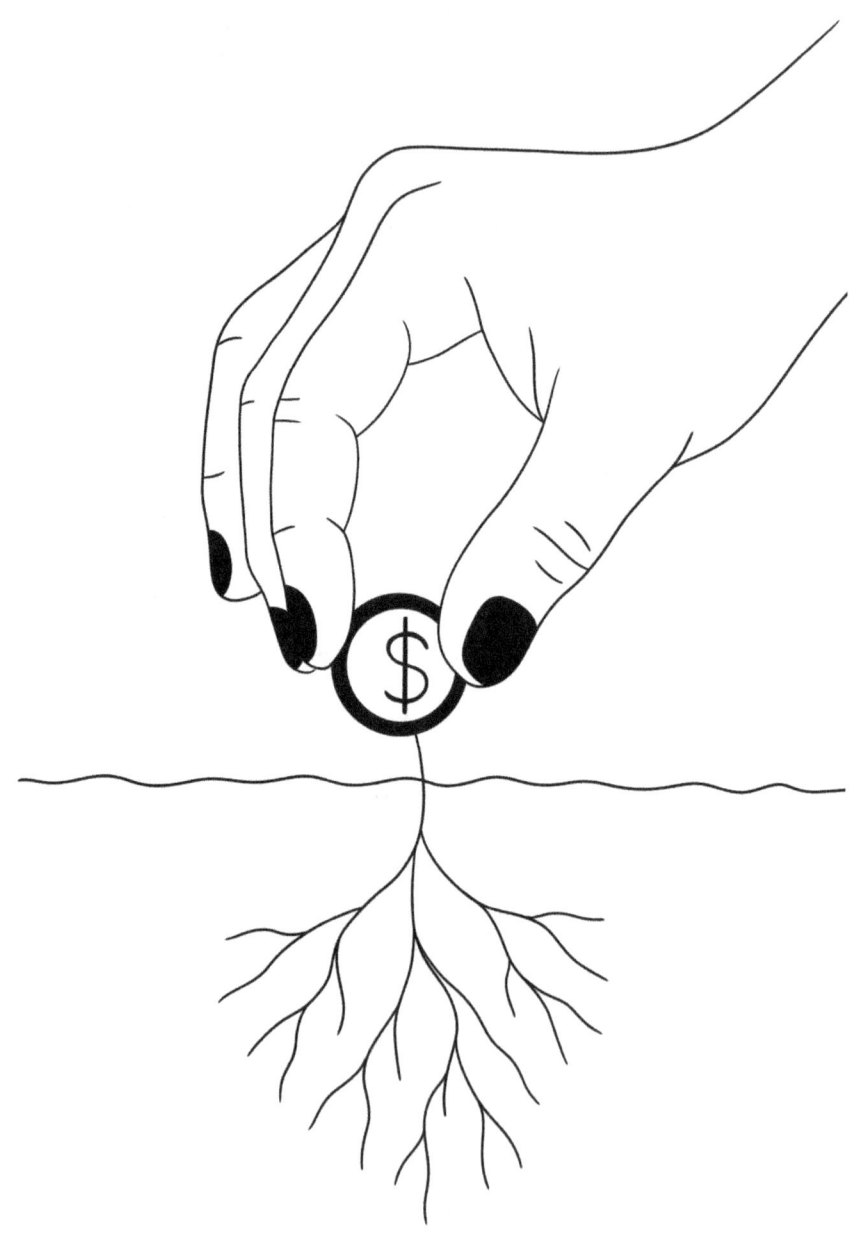

WALTER

A silver coin,
hidden in the kitchen drawer.
"Bless this house," it whispers.

> *I tried to hold onto those words*
> *as you painted mine*
> *in something darker.*

I remember the homecoming parade,
our backs pressed against church grass.
Bands played,
girls waved,

Walter called,
as I had prayed.

> *We had just placed an offer,*
> *for his house on School Drive.*
> *We came in well below his listing price.*
> *He said "you do what you need to,*
> *for that blessing of a family of yours.*
> *I'll do what I need to do for mine."*

Walter had always been
like a grandfather to me.

When I was young
It was frequent
We would sing together in choir,
One year, I was the "Christmas Star"
During rehearsals,
I would playfully wag my finger at him
"shame on you"
I still see him smiling back.

We would then continue to sing
"When he closes a door,
he always opens a window for us all."

While moving out,
of School Dr.
Walter fell down the basement stairs.

I guess I wasn't the only one
to take that trip.
I should have seen that as a bad Omen.

When we made it to closing,
Walter filled our hearts
with stories of the life
God provided he and his wife
on School Drive.

I couldn't wait to begin mine.

I thought this house was a blessing.
Just as the coin had referenced.
Anything broken,
would soon be mended.
I soon came to learn it was a curse.

The day we dug our fence,
Walter's wife was put in a hearse.

If Walter was alive today,
and saw the things you have done—
to his house,
to his yard,
to his **Christmas Star**—

I think he'd sternly
wag his finger,

"Shame on you."
And I can't pretend to imagine
what else he might say.

EIGHTEEN TWENTY-NINE

Eighteen
Twenty-Nine.
Those were our ages.
When we met.

Shame on me,
for falling for it.
Shame on you,
for everything else.

I really believed
I was mature for my age.

That was bullshit.

Looking back
I can see
how it all was just a ploy.

Now,
Being twenty-nine.
I can very clearly say
I would never find
interest in someone
who was as young
as I.

> *Was it my naivite?*
> *or my innocence?*
> *that made me the perfect prey?*

> *You were able to mold me into*
> *whatever you wanted me to be.*
> *Once you found*
> *a single flaw,*
> *you could use it to*
> *continually manipulate me.*

No I wasn't perfect.
In the beginning of our relationship,
I was young
in college.
I admit,
I messaged other guys
through facebook.
You still weren't
divorced yet.
It should have been a red flag.

But you held onto that.
For almost 10 years,
Until the final time,
you would ever
lay a had on me.

It's still crazy to me
how every part
of our life had become
a tactic to manipulate someone.

Our marriage
So you could get custody
of your eldest son
Why else would we have gotten married at the court house
Four days before your custody trial had begun?

Our daughter—
a pawn
before she even had a name.

A child support bill,
signed in my blood.

With each child
God blessed us,
you kept a tally—
more children,
more leverage,
more control.

You never wanted more kids.
You wanted more power.

I hate that I never saw it at eighteen.
But I do now,
at twenty-nine.

DOWN THE STAIRS

Do you remember that day?

I'm sure you do.
The morning after,
the walk of shame—
call it what you may.

Giggles and glee.
I lost my footing,
slid off the step.
As I stood back up,
I slipped again.

My goodness,
the jokes you made.

"No one would believe me

if you actually got hurt.

Are you okay?

People are going to think

I did this on purpose."

We laughed,
hysterically.
It became an inside joke.

The day I fell down the stairs.

Fast forward—six years.

There are no more "accidents."

Everything has changed.

No longer do
I lose my footing.
No—
it has been taken from me.

Instead of,

"No one would believe me,"
it's—

"No one would believe you."

Instead of,

"Are you okay?"
it's—

"Don't you dare let anyone see that bruise."

It's crazy,
how you foreshadowed
exactly what you would do.

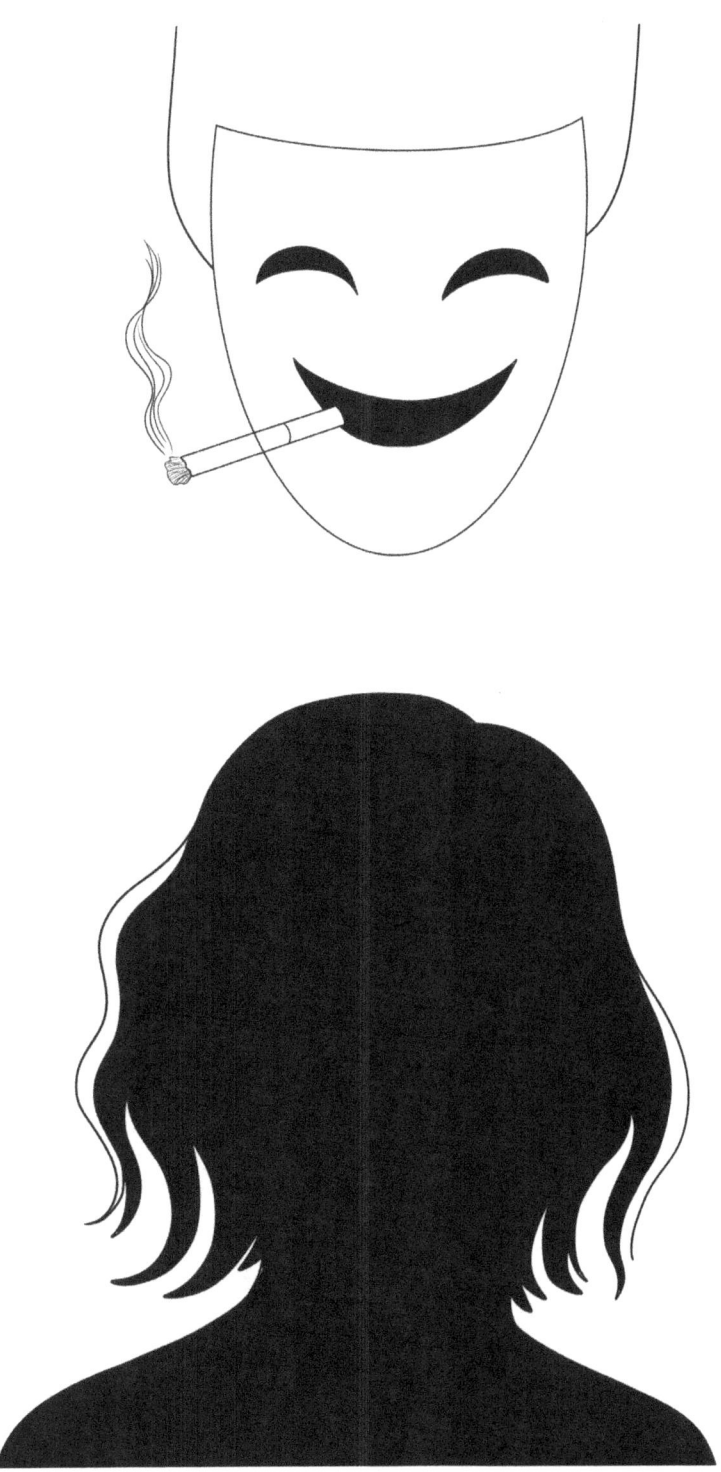

ALL GLORY TO THE MOST HIGH

You made us pose in the front yard that day.
May 10, 2022.

Before we went to coach a T-ball game,
you posted to social.

"All Glory to God Most High."

But you were high too.

You got mad at me.
My mom never liked your post.

You put on your hat,
played your role.
An exhausting character,
but you played it well,
for everyone else.

I was two months post-partum.
Like my body,
that shirt I wore was new.

When T-ball ended,
you insisted—Home Depot.
More shrubs, more trees—
yet again.

Regardless that it was 9 p.m.
on a school night.
The kids were tired.
So was I.

I obliged.

You got high.

The kids and I waited for you in the car.
You came back,
wanted Wendy's.

So I drove.

As I passed the food to the kids,
you ridiculed me
for not asking for help.

I shouldn't have to ask.

You struck me across the face.

Then blamed me.

I made you do it.

It was my fault
the children saw.

You said
I made you lose your appetite.

And again—

you got high.

As I drove home,
you continued.

Ridicule.
Verbal assault.

We reached the house.

I took the kids inside,
showered them all.
I said prayers,
put the girls to bed.

You stayed outside,
getting high.

I came downstairs with the baby.

You asked if I wanted to eat.
You said you calmed down.

I sat at the kitchen table,
baby in my arms,
breastfeeding.

He starts to spit up.

A common baby thing.
We've had four by now.
You should be used to this.

You start yelling—

Help him.

Take care of him.

I already am.

You scream at me—

You're letting him choke!

He's going to die!

But that is not what's happening.

He's just a baby.

Spitting up.

By the time you finish yelling,
he has already finished working through it.

I go to stand.

You get angrier.

I sit back down.

You accuse me—

Running away from you.

I try to explain.
I was going to change his clothes.

He's covered in spit-up.

"You always have a reason
for whatever you're doing.
You're always trying to change your story."

"I just wanted to sit down
and eat a meal with my wife,
but I'm not important enough to you!"

"You're always worrying
about everything else
rather than the man
standing right in front of you
who wants to be with you!"

"You're such a bitch!"

You scream at me.

I tried explaining—
you had just screamed at me
to take care of our son,
so that's what I was doing.

But that's when you came after me.

I was sitting in the chair,
holding our son.

You attacked—
pushed me,
the baby,
the chair.

Straight back.

I couldn't brace myself.
Couldn't stop the fall.

All I could do—
wrap my arms tight
around my baby.

Seconds passed.

My heart stopped
because he didn't cry.

But he was breathing.

He put himself to sleep.

I shielded him
from this belligerent assault.

I got up—
you came after me again.

I ran upstairs.

From below,
you screamed profanities
for hours.

Surprise, surprise.

Again—
you got high.

Hours passed.
You cried.
Apologized.

I didn't believe you.
But I was scared.

If I don't play along,
what happens?

You asked me to prove
I still love you.

After what you'd done,
do you really think
that's what I want?

I told you no.
More than once.

But here you came again.

"I know you don't really love me."

"If I was someone else, you'd fuck me."

"I've never been what you wanted."

"I know you're just going to leave me."

"You're just a dumb whore anyway."

So, I submitted.

Not even 45 minutes passed.

Angry you
was back.

Talking about baseball,
some little boy on the team.

"He'd be great
if his parents put more effort in."

I agreed.

"Everyone's trying their best.
Both his parents work full-time jobs."

You lost your mind.

I almost lost my life.

You put the gun to my head.

Almost pulled the trigger.

Our son—
less than two feet away,
asleep in his bassinet.

I don't know how
I got that gun from you.

But I did.

I hid it.

I took the baby downstairs.
Tried to sleep in the recliner.

Until you decided
you had unfinished business.

You came downstairs.

Dragged me off the recliner
by my feet.

"I'm going to be the abusive person
you want everyone to believe I am."

You pulled me out the front door
by my ankles—

while I was breastfeeding our son.

When I stood up,
you started punching me in the face.

Non-stop.

You wouldn't quit.

You kept saying
I deserved it.

I held our son.

I couldn't defend myself.

Because I was protecting him.

You went back inside.
Locked the door.

Left me
and our son
on the porch.

An hour passed.

4 a.m.

For the first time,
I was in peace.

Until you came back outside.

Dragged me in
by my hair.

You stood me
in front of the mirror.

Forced me to look.

"I don't love this woman."

"Look how stupid you look."

"You did this to yourself."

"I fucking hate you
for making me do this."

"You're going to get yourself
and that baby killed."

"That baby isn't mine—
and you're both going to die
if you don't quit this shit."

"You're not leaving this house
until the bruises are gone."

"The kids aren't going to school."

But—

All Glory to the Most High.

THE JOINT VENTURE

In 2021,
I accepted a role
*in a **Joint Venture.***

This job was everything—
everything I wanted.

I had potential,
a seat at the table.

You hated that I was thriving.

I was working
at the executive level,
exactly where I
was meant to be.

On my first day,
you called me upstairs—

"Never think

I'm intimidated by your career

or your coworkers."

On my second day,
you ripped my sweater,
pushed me down the stairs.

I had been on video calls,
introducing myself.

I told my boss—
I have a husband,
children,
we all have names
that begin with A.

                    He told me—
            his fiancée is a trauma nurse
                    at UCLA.

                                        But I was flirting.

I was such a whore.

                    From that day on,
                I was scared to do my job.

                                        I feared speaking.
                                        I feared smiling.
                                            Definitely—

DO NOT LAUGH.

                    I had learned my lesson.

                                            I was scared
                                    you would retaliate.

One mistake.
That's all it took.

                    I told you my boss
            planned to expand my role,
                overseeing all areas
                of the Joint Venture.

                                    He said I had the skillset.
                                    He said I could thrive.

29

You said—

> *"I always tell you this,*
> *but you don't listen to me*
> *because I'm not*
> *a rich white man."*

> *Maybe I didn't listen*
> *because I never knew*
> *how soon your kindness*
> *would turn to pain.*

I was always afraid
to do my job.

> *Eventually—*

the Joint Venture dissolved.

I still carry the weight.

> *Maybe we could have convinced them*
> *to renew the contract—*

> *if I could have done my job.*

Unafraid.

FRONT YARD PICTURE FRAME

Hose in hand,
there you stand,
day after day—
just spray away.

> *You line the perimeter,*
> *thick with wildflowers,*
> *sunflowers, and more.*
> *You plant apple trees,*
> *dogwoods,*
> *lush grass seeds—*
> *no one dare disturb*
> *your perfect, beautiful scene.*

You're always scared—
of what others may say,
of what others may see.

> *Forget keeping up with the Joneses—*
> *you're in competition*
> *with an 85-year-old*
> *senile man,*
> *God rest his soul.*

Don't play here,

Don't walk there.

Don't touch that.

This yard was suppose to be theirs.
It's turned into your art project.

                                        The kids,
                            quickly became afraid,

Because when they do,
and you know they will,

                                          play there
                            —you push them out of the way.
                          How dare they ruin your crafted display.

and when they walk there
—you slap the back of their head.
"I said get out of there."

                              and when they touch that
                        — you bark "are you fucking dumb
                              I told you not to do that"

But they're kids. It's what they do.
It's their yard.

                                    We had a dog once,
                                      Poor Daisy Mae.
                            You couldn't stop beating her.
                            Because she'd eat your grass.

She'd dig holes
and you'd put holes in her head.

Our oldest daughter asked me one day
Mommy why does daddy love the grass anyway?
it's like all he ever did was water the grass?
Doesn't he love us too?
We need watered too.

Hose in Hand
There you stand
day after day
just spray away.

If walls could talk &

floors could cry

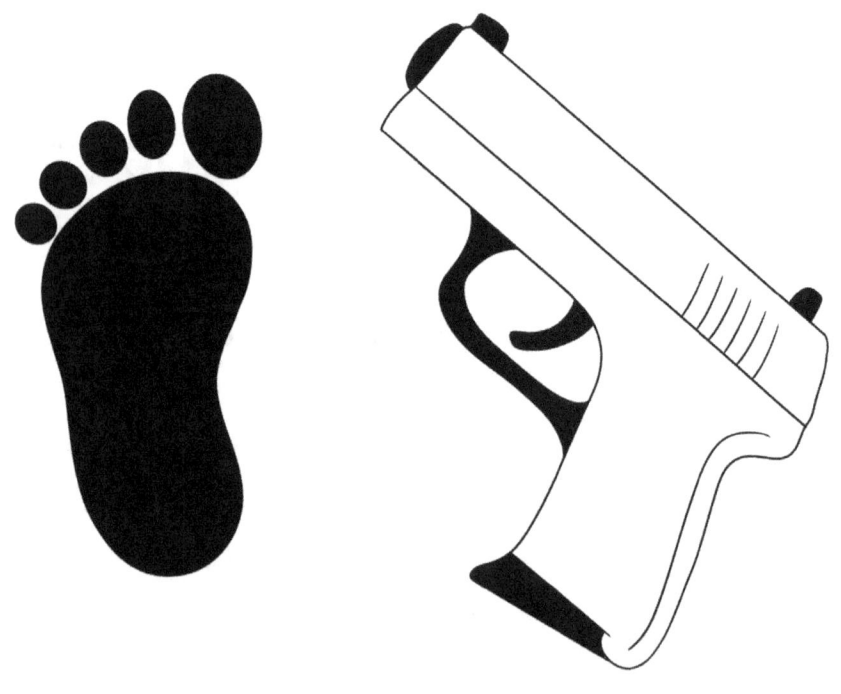

THE FIRST TIME

There we stood.

                              I can't recall
                             what led us
                        to these footprints.

The children,
just feet away,
Blippi playing
in the background.

                             I feel the hum
                           of the fridge.

You reach up,
grab the handgun.

I beg you to stop.

                            Black in your eyes.
                             Tears in mine.

"The kids will hear."

"You're being dramatic."

                             You hold the gun
                           to your own head.

I'm being dramatic.

You say
you don't want to hurt me,
you're doing this

for me.

> *I beg you not to.*
> *I reach for the gun.*

Your hands—
on mine.

Twisting.

Wow, that hurts.

"What are you doing?"

"Oh my God."

"You're breaking my fingers."

"Stop."

> *You say*
> *I'm making you do this.*

> *What?*
> *How?*

"Babe!"

"Please!"

"STOP!"

"THIS HURTS!"

You shove me.

I crash into the counter.

The kids hear.

"Mommy, are you okay?"

Mommy's fine.

Keep watching Blippi.

I love you.

I answer happily,
choking on tears.

You stand over me.

Hands—
tight
around my throat.

"Never try to stop me again."

I lay there,
in the kitchen corner.

Ten seconds.

Then I stand.

Shake it off.

Return to being Mom.

You walk upstairs.

Probably got high.

And that—
was the first time.

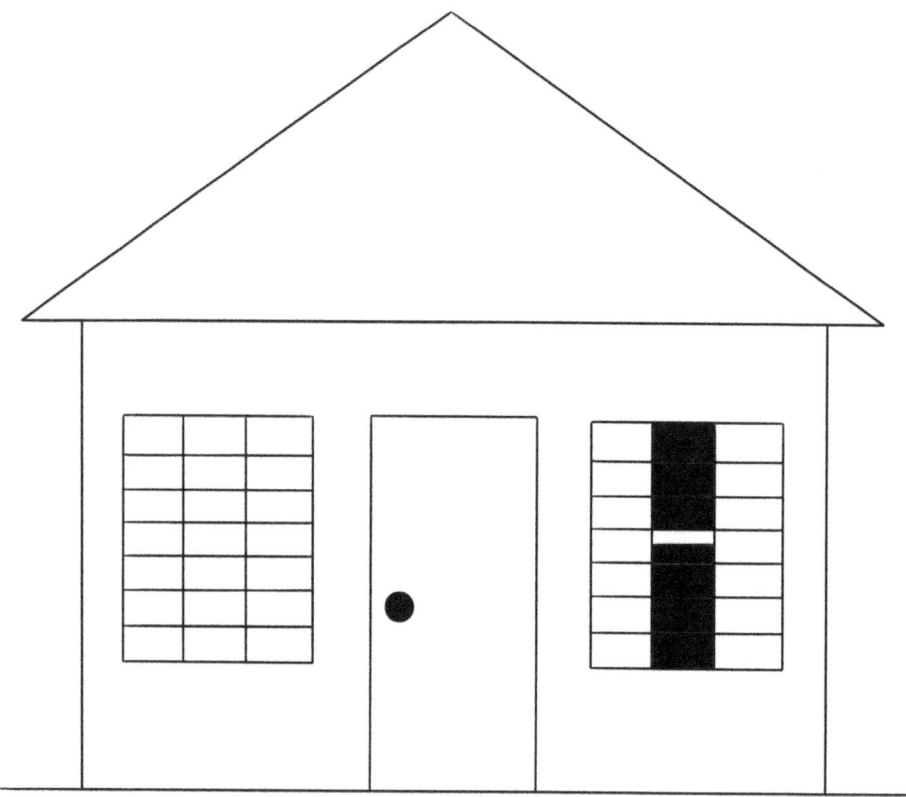

40

WINDOWS

Like a fear of day,
you hid each room away.

Curtains, blankets, jackets—
draped over every portal,
not a single one
left unbothered.

I always found it strange.

"Peeping Toms," you said.

"Spies."

"You never know who's watching."

Paranoia,
or something else?

The truth was,
you were just afraid
someone might see.

*See **you.***

See what you were.
See what you did.

Today—

I live in a house
where I broke all the blinds,
stripped every curtain,
and leave the lights on.

Night and day.

The only thing I fear—

is my fate
if one night,
I pass by the window,

and I see your face.

KITCHEN TABLES

In September of 2020,
we bought a table—
rustic, wooden, beautiful.

Five chairs, a bench,
room for ten.

$3,000.

I loved my kitchen table.

So much space—
for homework and lessons,
for baking cookies,
for rolling tamales.

The kids and I—
together,
right at this table.

But soon,
the memories soured.

You forced the kids to eat.
Belittled them.
Called them names.

Their first bully
sat at the head of the table.

Your hands slammed against the wood,
shaking our plates,
our bodies,
our trust.

If someone didn't submit
to your drug-induced commands,
the table would feel your rage.

You drove wedges
between your own children—
because they had different mothers.

And when I cooked—
you refused to eat.
Told the kids not to either.

You convinced them—
I had poisoned the food.

There—
at the table—
you assaulted me,
again and again.

Knocked me off my chair,
pushed me against the wood.

And the memory they still talk about—
the day before your last arrest.

You were screaming.
The girls were seated,
preparing for online school.
They were crying—
you told them to shut up.

This time,
I didn't back down.

You didn't like that.

And then,
you were gone.

Arrested.

I left with the kids.

I wanted to take my kitchen table,
but I couldn't.

I loved my kitchen table.

But there were two deep marks
on its surface.

And I couldn't bear to see them.

Because one look—
and I was back.

Sitting at that table.
So were you.

Your back to the kitchen sink.
Eyes black—
to match your soul.

A chef's knife in your hand,
blade gleaming.

Threats spilling from your mouth.

Then—

you stabbed the knife into the table.
Dragged it across the wood.

Once.

Twice.

Three times.

Drooling as you screamed,
like a rabid dog.

I loved my kitchen table.

Now, it's 2025.

My kitchen table is small.

There isn't enough space
for two people—
let alone me
and four kids.

It was given to me
by a shelter
for abused women.

But this table—
this one is safe.

And I am learning
to love my kitchen table again.

A FRONT PORCH CONFESSION

I've grown to hate my front porch.

One day in July,
swollen with life,
I sat beside you on the porch bench.

You were always paranoid.

A car passed down the road—
you were convinced
they were coming for us.

"A drive-by."

That doesn't happen here.

But I must have made a face
you didn't like.

I have a flaw—
I can control my mouth,
but not my expressions.

That flaw
accounted for 80%
of my bruises.

"You don't trust me."

"You think I'm crazy—
just like everyone else."

Do me a favor—
research the statistics
of drive-by shootings
in Hempfield Township.

You locked me outside.

Said I needed to **"act right."**

It was nearly 100 degrees.
I was nine months pregnant.

I was working.
You had no job.

No water.
No food.

Our daughters,
two and three,
pressed their faces
against the screen door,

"Mommy."

They cried.
You scolded them.

You didn't let me back inside
until your back hurt.

You needed my help.

Of course,
I helped you.

At the top of the stairs,
a ringing in my ears—

the world went black.

When I woke,
you said you needed to go
to the ER.

I called my mom
for the girls.

I put myself aside.

I drove you.

When I gave birth to my daughter,
she was blind in one eye.

The doctors said,

"No verifiable cause."

But every time
I look at that front porch,
I wonder—

if I hadn't been locked outside
that day,

would my baby girl still be blind?

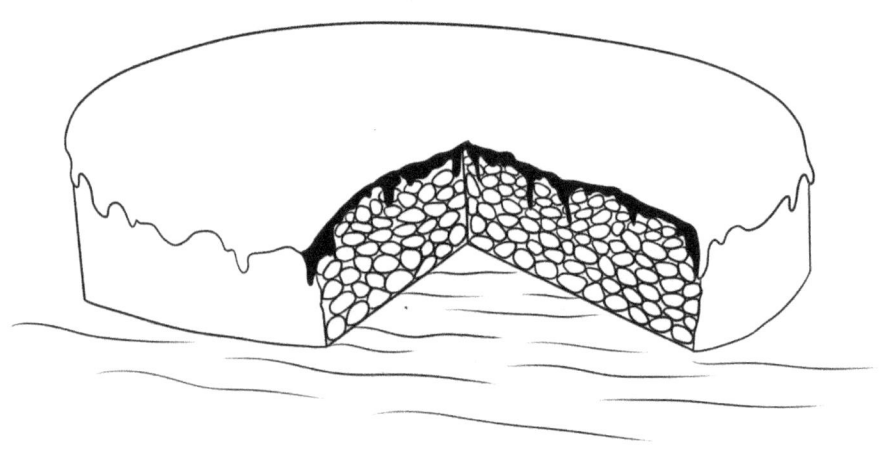

RIVER ROCKS OVER RIBBONS

Balloons and banners,
orange and blue.
Streamers strung
across the front porch, too.

Presents and cake.
My family came.

But you—

glued to your lava rock,
unmoving, untouched,
obsessed with perfection
no one asked for.

As our daughter shredded
wrapping paper,
your shears sliced through
landscaping linen.

We sang Happy Birthday.

The river rock pounded the ground,
a rhythm of stone against silence,
drowning us out.

The kids began to play.

You called for them
to work.

"Come here."

"Pick that up."

"Move this."

It's her third birthday.

You're being a jerk.

I fear if I stay,
this poor girl—

will never know

her true worth.

TRIANGLES

Just as a triangle has sides,
You do too.
The one everyone outside knows.
The one your family
2500 miles away loves.
The one we,
caged in these walls fears.

That morning I walked her up

to the doors of her school.
Her curls bounced as her feet danced.
And I laughed.
As I returned to the car I already knew
which side of you
would be greeting me.
Accosting and Accusing me.

We'd return to our home.

Where you would discipline me.
My Crime?
Smiling.

Side 1

You would begin with words.
Oh, how they would hurt.
I never let that show.
I washed those off.

When I emerged from the shower,
you knew your words had no power.
You began your accusations.
I stonewalled.

"Would You like me to Iron your clothes for tonight?"

Side 2

Next came your hands.
Around my throat.
Against my face.
These hurt too.
They always left marks.
Various shades of purple and blue.
Purple was my favorite color before you.
Once you left I began to Iron your clothes.
Our eldest had his band recital tonight.

You return again.
You could never leave anything alone.

Side 3

This time it was the iron.
Seared into my skin.
I still carry that triangle with me everywhere.

The outer side of you debuts.
We go support our son.

Your third and final side even makes an appearance,
as you make a call to your parents.

You're really supporting all of these angles,
to your demented triangle.

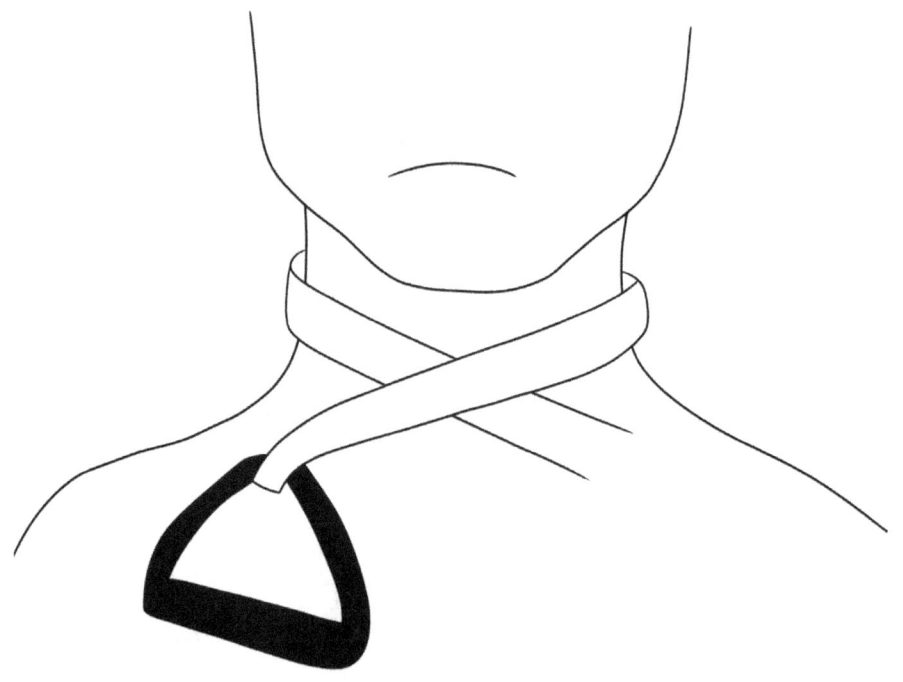

EXERCISE BAND

An exercise band.

Around my neck.
On the kitchen floor.

Seven months pregnant.

You thought our son
wasn't yours.

You tightened your grip—
not just on the band,
but on the story
you needed to believe.

I gasped,
hands clawing at rubber,
at air,
at reason.

I never broke our vows.

But you—

you broke everything else.

3/16

His Due Date was 4/5/22
his older sisters 5th birthday.
The induction was scheduled
for 3/29/22.
I always had issues with Kidney Stones.

This stories more painfull.
Forgive me if it's not written as beautifully in prose.

Your sick obsession with the lawn.
You had been planting shrubs,
lining up lava rocks,
designing fairie gardens
and laying out river rock.

It was 3/16
ironic huh?
You called me outside to see the work you had done.
I was tired.
Pregnant.
With your son.

As I stepped across the newly laid rock,
I steadied myself on the tree.
not your hand,
you had extended for me.
I didn't see it
under the dimly lit scene.

fragile male ego,
doesn't begin to describe it.
You began to go on.
I don't trust you.
I never look for you.
I don't appreciate the work you were doing.
the words quickly turned.
Before I knew it
we were in the kitchen by the basement door.
You were pushing me down the stairs.
while holding me up by my hair.
continually kicking me.

You let go of my hair.
I fall down the stairs.
The door slams.
Click.
Here I stay.

But I'm feeling more.
More than just sore
from the assault I've endured.
These feelings are familiar.
I've felt this tightness before.
This burning in my back.
The shortness in my breath.
Oh shit.

Come on, Calm Down Amanda. Just Breath.
It's Okay,
You Can do this.
Calm Down.
You're Baby's Going to Be Okay.
Just Breathe Amanda.
You Got This.
Breathe....
Breathe...
BREATHE DAMNIT!
....
....
Okay....
let's try to get back in the house.

I leave through the basement door.
As I walk up the front porch step
I peek in through the window
I see you laying on the couch..

I open the front door,
holding my breath.
fearing I may trigger you more.

You jump to your feet.
instantly start to scream.

I timidly begin to apologize.
what for?
I don't know.
I've done nothing wrong.

But I'm willing to admit fault.
To smoothe things over
and move forward.
You're not willing to accept it.
I tell you
I'm in labor.
Our baby is coming.
You telll me I'm doing this for attention
so that I can get out of trouble.

I assure you that this is not what this is.
You tell me i just want you to feel bad.
I try to get you to believe me.
You wont
You tell me you hate me.
Shut up.

instead, I call my mom.

She takes me to the hospital.
That full moon night
3/16,
"God so loved the world he gave his only son"
I was in labor with mine.

MY LUCKY CHARM

I was in labor for hours.

My mother stayed with me,
while you were home
with the girls.

You called me once—
to tell me I was lying.

Twice—
to call me a whore.

Three times—
to cuss out my mother,
for "covering for me"
while I got my epidural.

Hours passed.

You refused to join me,
refused to acknowledge
I was in labor.

Then, suddenly—
you insisted my mother
take the girls,
so you could come.

Like it was your choice.

This was the worst labor

ever.

I heard you call your mom.

"She's acting so miserable."

"I don't know why I'm even here."

"She's just laying here, resting."

MOTHERFUCKER—
I'M IN LABOR,
DRUGGED UP ON PITOCIN.

And every few minutes,
you stood over me,
casually reminding me—

as soon as this baby is born,

if he's Black,

you were going to murder him.
And me.

Good thing I didn't have to worry.

But man—
that is a different type of torture.

Lying on a table,
trapped in my own body,
while a man
stands over me,
threatening to kill me,
kill my baby,
the moment he is born—

based on a delusion.

You believed—
last year,
when I went to the police,
I hooked up with an officer
at the barracks.

Yes, picture it now—

"Oh, sir, my husband won't stop beating me.

I don't want you to arrest him.

No, but—

will you please put it in me?

Let's give him another reason to hit me."

And here we are,
nine months later.

Because that's the type of person
I am, right?

And the skin color—

solely based on

a high school boyfriend.

Can we say insecurity?

Then, I delivered our son.

On St. Patrick's Day.

My Lucky Charm.

And something shifted.

Or maybe,
it didn't.

You cried
when you saw him.

I didn't trust you.
I didn't want you
to touch him.

You cried.
Apologized.

You said you'd be different.

"He changed me."

I used any excuse
to send you away.

"Go to Target."

"Get me a onesie."

"Bring me coffee."

"Please—just leave."

Get out of my room.

I wish I had been strong enough
to rip one of those red tabs.

But I was scared.

I'll admit it.

I was too scared then.

On the drive home,
you started fighting
with your mom and dad.

You didn't talk to them
for months.

You told me not to, either.

I still sent them pictures
of the baby,
behind your back.

The kids were at our house,
with my parents.

But you had me tell them—

"Don't stay."

So they left
as soon as we got home.

We didn't see them
for two months after that.

Because of what you said
to my mom
that day
on the phone.

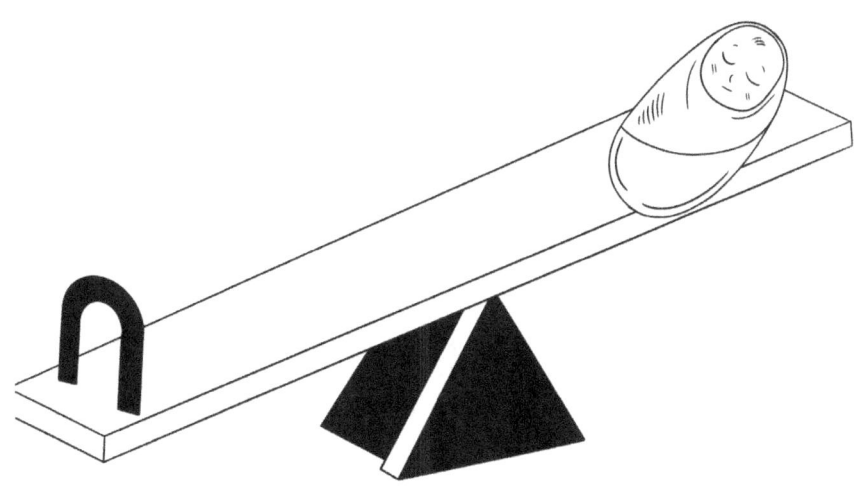

BLUE SEASAW

Sitting in the grass,
playing with the baby.

He's balancing
on the little blue seesaw,
not even old enough to walk yet.

I am distracting myself—
from your most recent attack.

Your words,
I can defend.

But I have asked you,
time and time again—

Please, stop.

Stop coming after
who I am as a person.

Since the very first time,
at the bottom of my parents' drive,
after you admitted
what you had done
to my father—

we went to talk.

I asked you then—

72

***Why does every little thing
always circle back
into a personal attack?***

*You looked at me,
shrugged,
and said—*

*"I can't help it.
My mental conditions
won't allow me
to do that."*

What the fuck is that?

I snap out of my head.

*I come back—
to see my little baby,
laughing with glee,
bouncing and rocking.*

And then—

you.

*Oh no.
Here you come.
What will you say now?*

*I bite my tongue,
let you spit your words.*

*You keep going,
pushing harder,
getting angrier.*

I ignore you.

Focus on my baby.

Then—

You kick me over.

*In the front yard,
for all to see.*

*And then,
you begin to scream.*

"Leave me alone."

"Please."

"Please."

"Please."

This isn't a **Sabrina Carpenter song.**

*I just want to play
with my son*

in peace.

But no—

You can't do it.

*You get louder.
More violent.*

Telling me—

I *am the one
making the scene.*

74

I take our son inside.

You follow.

Hitting.
Shoving.
Still screaming.

I am holding the baby,
for God's sake.

I try to make it
to the steps.

You grab my arm.

"Don't walk away from me."

I don't owe you anything.

Why won't you let me leave?

GROW OLD WITH ME

Behind slammed doors
beneath a sign that reads
"Grow Old With Me,
The Best is Yet to be"

inches away from me
your spit finds its way
to my face.
A knife clenched within your fist.
"STOP FUCKING WITH ME"

Once again—a familiar scene.
you tell me I'm doing something
I reassure you I'm not doing anything.
You continue to scream.
demanding I take accountability
for you turning into this being.

"IM GOING TO KILL MYSELF"
you shriek.

> *Please lets get you some help.*
> *babe, let's put the knife down.*

"NO, SHUT UP AMANDA.
IF YOU DON'T SHUT UP I WILL CUT MYSELF.
You're such a bitch,
You do this all the time.
You've really ruined my life."

You scream as you shove me
into the second story window.

I fall to the ground.
I get back to my feet..
But I've moved too fast.
Now I have triggered you more..

You begin to kick me in the leg.

This time I stay down.

"You're too stupid to get up.
You want to stay down.
You want to play the victim.
You want to be hurt.
You pathetic weak little girl."

I still feel your words.

"Did you pay attention to where I was kicking?
I was aiming for your tattoo.
maybe it would summon your papaw from the grave
and he would knock some sense into you,
he'd see how pathetic you are."

Babe can you please stop?

"I SAID SHUT UP OR I'M GOING TO CUT MYSELF
DON'T YOU REALIZE MY BLOOD WILL BE ON YOUR
HANDS!?"

Babe please put the knife down.

Cut 1.

Blood drips.
"Can't you see I'm terrified of you!?
STOP DOING THIS TO ME!
YOUR GOING TO KILL ME!"

Babe please stop.

Cut 2.

"SHUT THE FUCK UP YOU FUCKING BITCH."

Cut 3.

Joining your blood and tears
You fall to the floor

you scream that I did this to you.
Your blood is now on my hands.

I grab a t-shirt from the drawer,
tie it around your arm.

Holding myself and your wound together
I'm blocking all emotions out.

You push through me,
as if nothing happened
then I hear the water begin to run..

about 4 minutes pass
you yell and ask
for me to bring you a joint
and hydroxizine.

you make sure to remind me
how calm you are in this situation
and how panicked I am.

because your "trained" for this.
The Best is Yet to Be?
I don't think I want to wait and see?

WHAT WAS YOUR JOB?

It was my responsibility
to pay the bills.

To wake the kids up.
Get them dressed.
Fed.
Ready for the day.

It was my responsibility
to pack school lunches.

To go grocery shopping,
to manage food inventory,
to make sure there was always
something to eat.

It was my responsibility
to take the kids to school.

To work from home.
To earn an income.

Not too much—
you feared if I made too much,
I'd leave you.

It was my responsibility
to change all the diapers.

To cook the food.
Or drive to pick up
whatever you were craving.

Some days,
I would cook—
only for you to throw it away,

because your paranoia
convinced you
I was poisoning us all.

It was my responsibility
to manage every doctor's appointment.

Even yours.

To pick up the kids from school.
To facilitate every after-school activity.

To keep you comfortable
at all times.

Massaging you.
Laying out your clothes
so you wouldn't have to look.
Anticipating your needs
before you even knew them.

It was my responsibility
to wash the clothes,
to wash the dishes,
to clean.

24/7.

But don't rush.
Don't move too fast.

That stresses you out.

And always smile.

It was my responsibility
to bathe the kids.
To get them ready for bed.

To prevent you
from being triggered.

I was supposed to be
your protector.

Funny,
how the roles
were reversed.

It was my responsibility
to keep you happy.

To keep the kids
happy,
healthy,
loved.

To make sure
you always had socks
and underwear.

To help the kids
anytime they needed anything.

To fix

everything
you broke.

TVs.
Dressers.
Beds.
Walls.

Feelings.

Hearts.

What was your job?

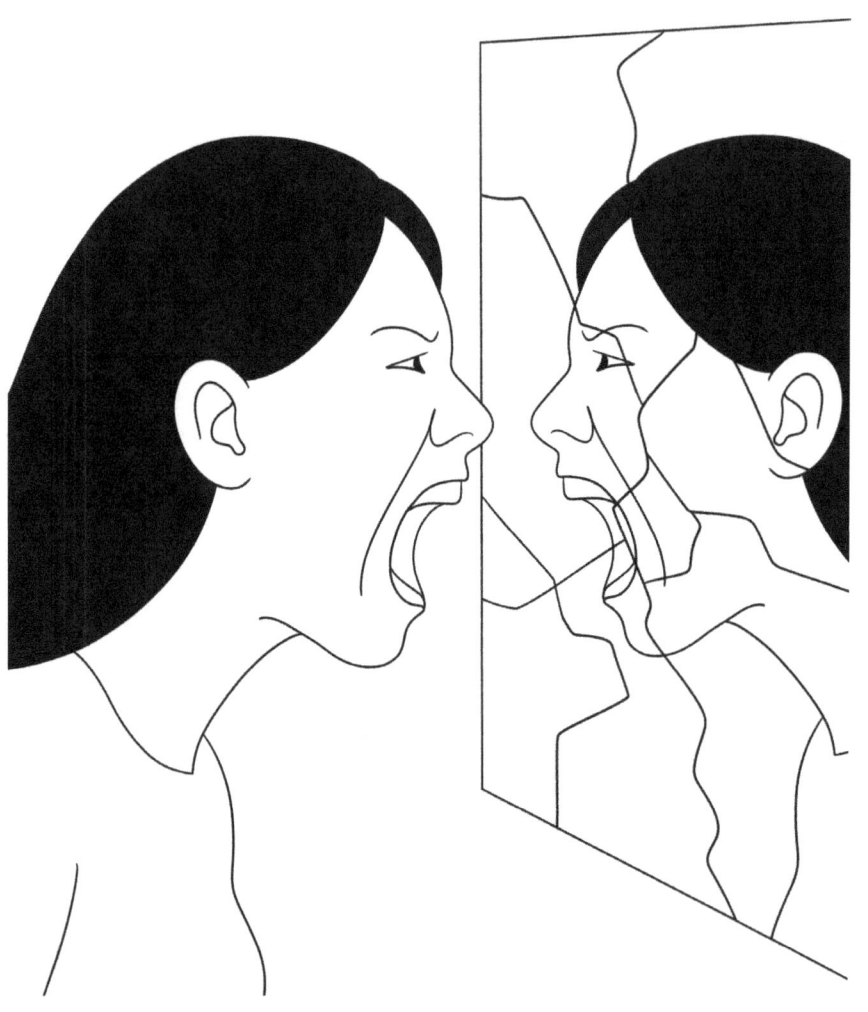

JUST FUCKING KILL ME

Steam seeps through
the shower door.

I've grown so tired—
of hearing the same words,
spewn at me,
again and again.

Repetitive in nature.
Lacking in appreciation.

I am the only one
who goes to work,
who feeds,
clothes,
bathes the kids,
changes the diapers.

Yet all I hear—

I don't do enough.

I'm a whore.

Your life would be better without me.

You were so successful before.

You wish I was dead.

And maybe—
you do.

You shove me
into the doorway.

My arm slams
against the frame.

Pain rushes up my bones,
but I don't even flinch.

I am too tired
for this.

Too tired for you.

So in my exhaustion,
I let out the words—

"Just fucking kill me, then."

After all,

isn't that what you want?

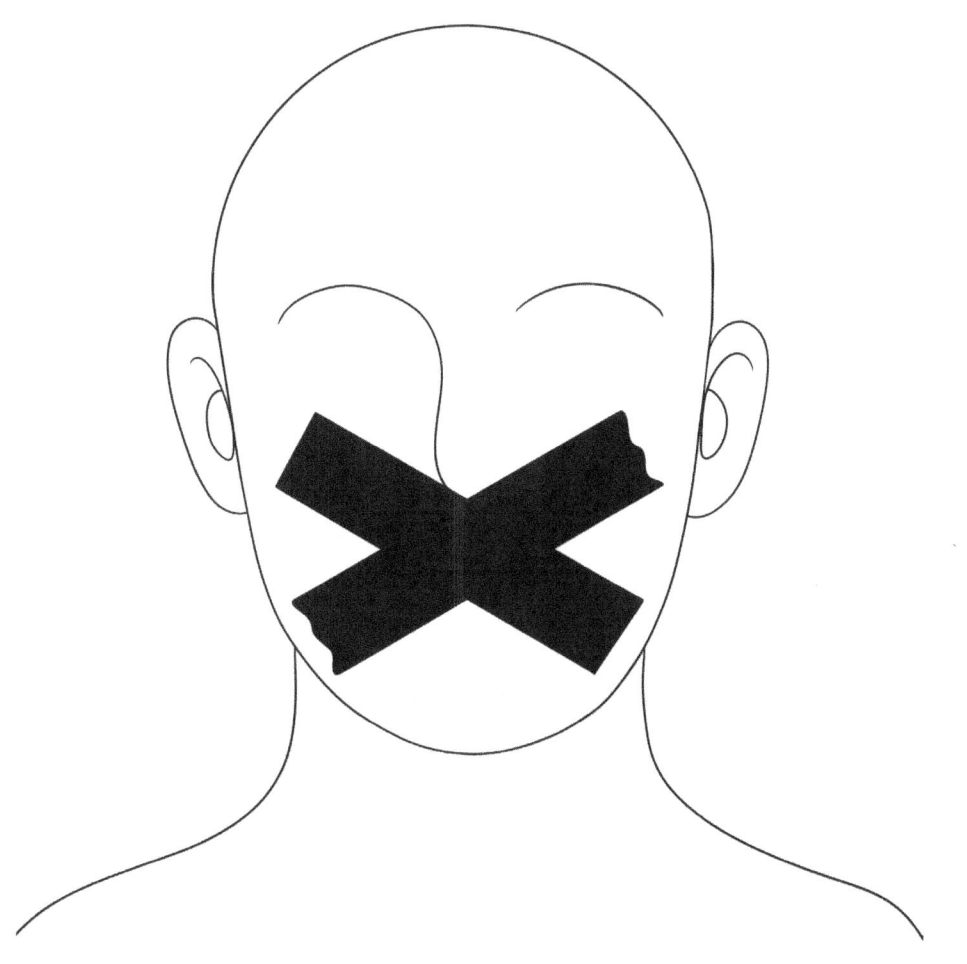

PAINTERS TAPE

Painters tape—

wrapped tight,
layered thick,
transformed into
brass knuckles.

Striking my face.

"Dude, are you okay?"

AMETHYST NECKLCE

The amethyst necklace
you gave me that day—
a reward for a job

not so well done,
you would say.

That morning,
you were sore.
And I was willing.

I massaged your legs,
your back,
trying to give you
the semblance of living.

Something I did was wrong.

What?

I don't know.

Too hard?
Too easy?

I'll never really know.

So you gave me
an amethyst necklace—

and hung my head
out our bedroom window.

The officer's words,
so harsh,
so clear—

"Well, you never stopped breathing, my dear."

"No one cares
if he threw a dumbbell
and it grazed your ear."

"Yes, I can see the necklace—

unfortunately,
he wouldn't even get a year."

You Reap
what you sow

THE DISEASE

When the disease began to consume me,
you quickly made it about you.

How it scared you.
How it affected you.

You cried—

"I see your color fading,"

"all your shades of gray."

You called my mother,
weeping into the phone.

"She's dying."

But tell me—

Why were you trying to kill me?

Why did you still beat me?

When the cops came,
you told them—

"No, she has a bleeding disorder.

That's why she has all the bruises."

You knew—
I couldn't clot.

The bleeding

could kill me.

But still,

you hit me anyway.

I got my diagnosis.

I was on my road to remission.
I was feeling better.

A few years passed.

New, terrifying words
began to surface—

Lymphoma.

Lupus.

Ouch.

This one's a little scary.

I went through the testing alone.

Yes, you were in the car.
Sometimes, you were even in the exam room—
but you said you had too much anxiety
to hold my hand.

But when it was time for the knife,
when they cut into me—

that was one I had to bear entirely alone.

And you know what?

You stood before our families,
playing your role—
the man who cared.

But behind the screen,
you told me—

"I hope it's true."

"I hope it's cancer."

Because—

"that's what you deserve."

I recall the times you said—

"This is God punishing you."

"For being so absurd."

"For being such a terrible person."

"You don't even deserve to be alive."

As you—

continued to beat the life out of me.

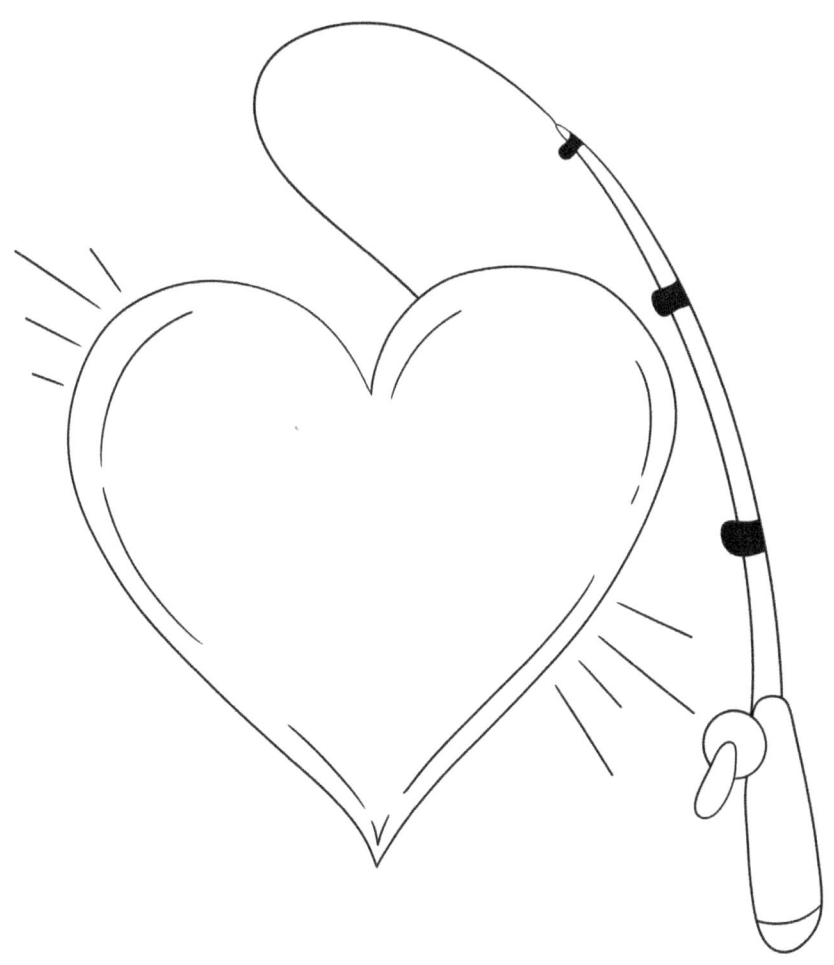

WAS THAT LOVE?

They say love
makes you do crazy things.

But what does hate make you do?

From the outside looking in,
I am certain—
nothing you ever did
was fueled by love.

Answer me.

Does love make you threaten
your pregnant wife?

Does love force her
to lock herself in the bathroom,
clutching her belly,
holding her breath,
as you pound on the door?

Was it love
that made you scream obscenities,
that made you torment her,

break her down to nothing?

Oh yes,
it must have been love—

that told her you would ram
a six-foot metal rod
so deep inside of her
that it would kill her unborn child.

You said
you would find pleasure in her screams.

You said
she, too, would die from blood loss.

You said
that baby—

your own blood—
was a bastard.

He deserved it.

Those were **your words.**

Was that love?

Was it love for your daughters
that made you tell them
you would murder their grandfather?

It was your voice,
your twisted imagination,
painting a picture
of their papaw—

his stomach split open,

his intestines falling to the floor,
right in front of them.

You told this
to our three- and four-year-old daughters.

Did you think
this was love?

Two years gone,
and now I know—

You are a being

incapable of love.

WONT BE THE CASE

Don't act like it was an accident
you didn't mean for it to happen
the way you treated our children
it was tragic.

At 2 years old
she would bawl,
you would tackle her.
I'll never forget that sight
in the hall.

I came through the door
there you were
on top of her
hand over her mouth to muffle her screams
all because she had a bad dream.
you blamed it on PTSD.
she wasn't even 3.

when out of your control,
their behaviors became
you'd resort to the insane.
there was the day .

infront of their face,
ages 3 and 4,
you cut the heads off of
all the toys and animals they adored.

my parents and I
as hard as we tried,
weren't able to locate a replica replacement
for each stuffy and toy that died.

You continually threatened them
with cruel words and baseball bats.

You'd shove them to the ground,
tell them it's their fault
their too stupid to stay standing on their feet
they wanted to fall.

You locked your daughter in a closet.

You kicked your son in the face.

By two years old,
he shouldn't know how the hardwood tastes.

Now you say you want custody,
that simply won't be the case.

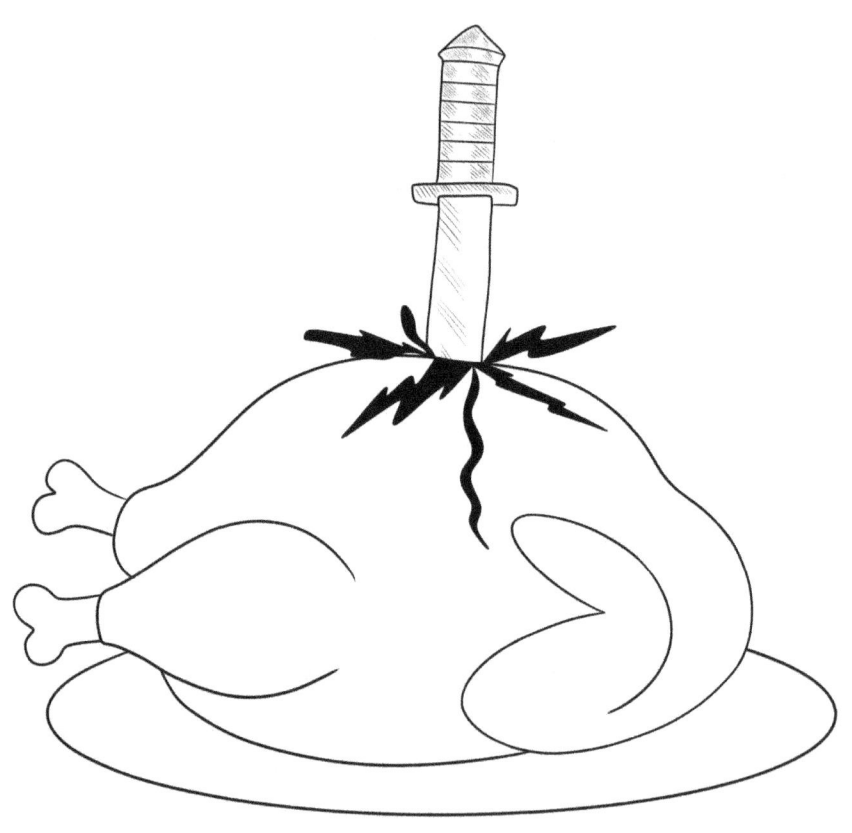

THANKSGIVING DAY

There's a recording on my phone
Five Minutes and Nine Seconds long.

Two Thousand Twenty Three
It's you screaming and beating.
This has been shared
with lawyers, judges and the guardian ad litem

Everyone has seen what you've done.

It's crazy to say Thanksgiving Day
because
some days I have to press replay to assure myself

I didn't make up the life I claim.

BEDR∞M BIRCH TREES

Walls Decorated with more than just
trade show and antique finds painted with cruel words

stained from blood and tears drywall
riddled with holes from dodged projectiles.

A single wall I elegantly designed Wall
papered white birch tress
that lined along side School Drive
this wall was my favorite.

When we designed this too,
you and I
we did this together
before your mask fell

and your touch became lethal.

when we picked out the paint
I loved navy blue.

maybe that's why you began
to paint it on me too.

I ordered the wall paper from target.
I was so excited.

The beautiful white birch trees
for our bedroom, as an accent.

It was perfect.

As I applied the wall paper
methodically,

I was 6 months pregnant.
I became frustrated.
Emotional.

I just needed a moment.

Your words quickly overwhelmed me.

I cried.

You made me feel worse.

I still feel all of that.

That desire to be perfect.

That need to not feel anything at all.
because feelings are wrong.

As years would pass,

every time we would drive
on the turnpike
we'd go through a section
thick with birch trees.

I always stare off,
disassociate.

You'd notice and make a comment.

You believed I must have "roots" to a local tribe nearby. maybe that's
true.

But I stare off wondering. wandering.

What would happen?
If I went missing in those white birch trees?

I'd probably be safer there
than under the branches in my own room.

Today he has a new woman
sleeping under my white birches.

I hope she's safer than I was.

BETTY

Her last breath—
we were out west.

It was unexpected.

Early June second.

You hadn't even met yet.

You were absent.
I was broken.

I reached—
for peace,
for closeness.

I drove off one night,
looking for something
to tether me to her.

Your accusations
welcomed me home.

Not sorrow.
Not comfort.

Accusations.

I was sitting
at my grandmother's table,
the one where we'd talk,
where she'd share wisdom,
history, love,
and Werther's caramels.

But no—
to you,
that's not what I was doing.

To you,
I was at another man's house,
stripping down,
giving my heart to him.

Two days after
my Mamaw's stopped.

Betty Needham—
you never got to meet him.

Whether you know it or not,

> ***you taught me***
> ***I don't need him.***

A MOTHER'S WISDOM

I over heard a mother once

tell her daughter

to be nicer to her boyfriend

ill tell mine to be meaner

to be firmer

set boundaries that are unwavered

by guilt trips or false accusations

           my mother used to say I needed to play hard to get

           i always felt it was such an odd thing to say.

           now I understand what she meant

           id tell my daughters the same thing

           dont play into his hand

           or else you'll fall victim

           to it

www.ingramcontent.com/pod-product-compliance
Lightning Source LLC
Chambersburg PA
CBHW070725130626

46553CB00005B/2145